PRESIDENTS OF THE U.S.A.

HARRY S. TRUMAN
OUR THIRTY-THIRD PRESIDENT

by Ann Graham Gaines

THE CHILD'S WORLD ®

The Child's World

Published in the United States of America

The Child's World®
1980 Lookout Drive • Mankato, MN 56003-1705
800-599-READ • www.childsworld.com

Acknowledgments
The Child's World®: Mary Berendes, Publishing Director

The Creative Spark: Mary McGavic, Project Director and Page Production;
Shari Joffe, Editorial Director; Deborah Goodsite, Photo Research

The Design Lab: Kathleen Petelinsek, Design

Content Advisers: Randy Sowell, Archivist; and Liz Safly, Library Technician;
Harry S. Truman Library, Independence, Missouri

Photos
Cover and page 3: White House Historical Association (White House Collection)
(detail); White House Historical Association (White House Collection)

Interior: The Art Archive: 19, 22 (Culver Pictures); Associated Press Photos: 17,
28, 34; The Bridgeman Art Library: 21, 23 (Private Collection, Peter Newark
American Pictures); Corbis: 15, 33 (Bettmann), 27, 29, 30, 36; Getty Images:
16 and 38, 31 (Time & Life Pictures), 20 (Getty), 26 (AFP); The Granger
Collection, New York: 10, 35, (The Granger Collection, New York) 32 (ullstein
bild-UPI); Harry S. Truman Library: 4, 5, 6, 7, 8, 12, 13 and 39 (Kansas City
Journal Post, Courtesy of Harry S. Truman Library), 37 and 39 (National Park
Service-Abbie Rowe, Courtesy of Harry S. Truman Library); iStockphoto: 44
(Tim Fan); Landov: 9 (Bill Greenblatt/UPI); SuperStock: 25 (SuperStock, Inc);
U.S. Air Force photo: 45.

Library of Congress Cataloging-in-Publication Data
Gaines, Ann.
  Harry S. Truman / by Ann Graham Gaines.
    p. cm. — (Presidents of the U.S.A.)
  Includes bibliographical references and index.
  ISBN 978-1-60253-061-4 (library bound : alk. paper)
 1. Truman, Harry S., 1884–1972—Juvenile literature. 2. Presidents—United
States—Biography—Juvenile literature. I. Title. II. Series.

  E814.G345 2008
  973.918092—dc22
  [B]

2008000524

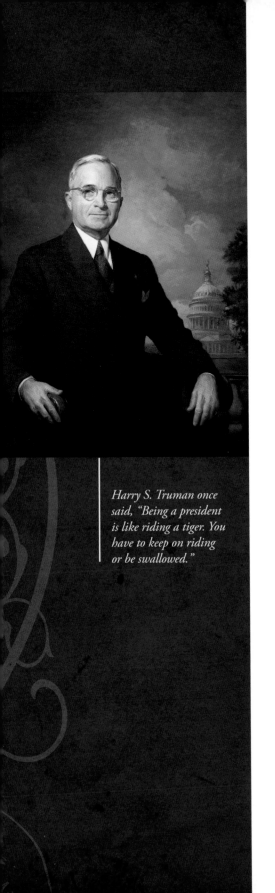

Harry S. Truman once said, "Being a president is like riding a tiger. You have to keep on riding or be swallowed."

TABLE OF CONTENTS

CHAPTER ONE

YOUNG TRUMAN

Harry S. Truman never wanted to become president of the United States. In 1944, he ran for election as vice president of the United States. He shared the political ticket with Franklin Delano Roosevelt, who was running for his fourth **term** as president. Truman was glad to serve his country, but he did not want to be in charge of it. He hoped that in 1948 he would be back where he'd been for twelve years, in the U.S. Senate. He liked being vice president because one of his duties was to **preside** over the Senate. He had made many friends in the Senate and enjoyed serving there. But everything changed just a few months after Roosevelt and Truman were sworn into office. On April 12, 1945, Roosevelt died. When a U.S president dies, the vice president automatically steps into office. Even though he did not want to be president, Harry S. Truman became one of our most important presidents ever.

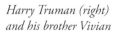

Harry Truman (right) and his brother Vivian

Harry Truman's father, John Anderson Truman, was born in 1851. Harry's mother, Martha Ellen Young Truman, was born in 1852. In the 1840s, both of their families had moved from Kentucky to Westport, Missouri.

Harry S. Truman started out in life as a farm boy. He was born on May 8, 1884, in Lamar, Missouri. Harry's father, John, earned his living by selling livestock—horses and mules. The fenced lot where he kept the animals sat just across the street from the Trumans' house. This allowed John to spend a lot of time with his family. Harry's mother, Martha, took care of their home. This was not easy because their house had no electricity or running water. She cooked on a wood stove and did their laundry outside in a tub.

John Truman's business never did very well. His family soon grew to include a second son, named

The Trumans had many relatives living in Missouri. Harry's grandparents, aunts, uncles, and cousins all lived in the same area. They visited each other often.

Harry had bad eyesight and needed thick glasses to be able to see well. "Without my glasses, I was as blind as a bat," he once said. The glasses were so expensive, his mother would not allow him to play rough sports. "I was kind of a sissy," Truman recalled.

Vivian, and a daughter named Mary Jane. In 1887, the Trumans went to live on Martha's parents' farm in Grandview, Missouri. In 1890, the family moved to the town of Independence. There the Trumans bought a big house on a huge lot. John Truman went back to selling livestock. He also continued to do some farming. He dug a vegetable garden at their new home. Martha's father had died, but her mother still lived on the farm in Grandview. John Truman continued to grow crops there, going back and forth between their house in the city and the farm in the country. He always gave his son Harry plenty of chores to do.

Harry enjoyed starting school in Independence. His mother had taught him to read before he even began school. By nature, he was a quiet boy. He admitted later that he was "kind of a sissy." Even so, he made many friends. One was a girl named Bess Wallace. Friends from the age of five, Harry and Bess graduated from high school together in 1901. By that time, Harry had grown to his full size. At five feet ten inches (178 cm) tall, he was a slim man with a ready smile.

Soon after high school, the Truman family left Independence. John Truman had lost all their money in a bad business deal. The Truman family had to sell their house. They moved to Kansas City, a big city, in the hopes John could find a new job there. Soon after,

John moved his family back to Martha's family's farm near Grandview and returned to the life of a farmer.

Harry had hoped to go to the United States Military Academy at West Point—the army's college, but his eyesight was not good enough. So after high school, he worked first for the Santa Fe Railroad and then as a bank clerk. He really liked living on his own in a boarding house in Kansas City. But in 1906, when his father asked him to come work on the farm, he agreed.

Harry Truman didn't love the life of a farmer, but he did the work well. A very organized man who paid

As a young man, Truman worked on his family's farm in Grandview, Missouri. Here he is driving a horse-drawn soil cultivator.

In 1905, Harry Truman joined the Missouri National Guard.

Truman fought bravely during World War I. He served for nearly two years before he was discharged in 1919.

attention to details, he figured out how to make their soil produce more crops. In his free time, he courted his old friend Bess Wallace. He bought a used car so he could drive to see her in Independence.

By 1914, John Truman had become their county's road overseer. One day he was out working on a road and tried to pick up a huge boulder. He hurt himself so badly he had to have surgery. Within a short time he died, leaving Harry in charge of the farm and the county roads. Harry also tried to find other ways to make money, investing first in a mine and then in the oil business. Neither made him rich.

The Great War, today known as World War I, broke out in Europe in 1914. Harry Truman had served in the Missouri National Guard from 1905 to 1911. When the United States entered the war in 1917, Truman rejoined the National Guard. His unit was called into active duty later that year. He believed it was the duty of the United States to help Great Britain, France, and Russia fight Germany and its **allies,** known as the Central Powers. He thought Germany must be stopped from expanding into an ever-more-powerful empire.

Truman had always liked studying the history of war. In the army, he could use what he had learned. He left for France in April 1918 and served there as

Soon after they married, Harry and Bess Truman moved into Bess's family home in Independence, Missouri. They lived there, on and off, until the end of Truman's life.

John and Martha Truman named their son Harry S. Truman. The "S" did not stand for anything. It was meant to honor both of Harry's grandfathers. It stood for both "Solomon," after his mother's father, and "Shipp," after his father's father.

an **officer.** His troops included tough men who liked to look for trouble, but they obeyed Truman. He was a good commander, and his men fought bravely. By November, the United States and its allies had won the war. The army stayed for a time to help establish peace, but in the spring of 1919, Truman and his men headed home.

Before he had left for war, Harry Truman had proposed to Bess. When he got back home, they promptly married, on June 28, 1919. In February of 1924, they had their only child, a daughter named Margaret.

BESS TRUMAN

Harry Truman met Elizabeth Virginia Wallace, his future wife, at Sunday school when they were young children. Bess, as she was called, was born in Independence, Missouri, on February 13, 1885.

Harry and Bess Wallace went to school together. She was a very active little girl. A friend remembered that Bess was the first girl she ever knew who could whistle through her teeth. Bess loved to ice-skate and play baseball and tennis. Harry wasn't nearly as good at sports as Bess was. He preferred to read or play piano, and his glasses made him look quiet and studious. Occasionally, Bess allowed Harry to carry her books home from school. Sometimes they studied together. But in school, they were just friends, even if Harry thought she was the prettiest girl in town.

Bess and Harry graduated from high school in 1901. Bess then went to a college for women in Kansas City. But when her father died in 1903, she returned home to be with her mother. Together with her three brothers, they moved into her grandfather's house. For the next 16 years, Bess helped her mother run the household. Then one day, Harry Truman took a trip to Independence. He and Bess renewed their friendship. They would see each other whenever possible until 1917, when they finally became engaged. They married when Harry returned from World War I in 1919.

When Bess Truman became the first lady, many Americans said she was the woman they most admired. She donated her time to many charitable causes. She was a quiet, gracious hostess, but she did not hold press conferences or grant interviews with reporters. Mrs. Truman always worked hard to be a good politician's wife. Even so, she was glad when her husband decided not to run for a third term as president. She could hardly wait to return to a quiet life in Missouri.

Mrs. Truman died in 1982 at age 97. In a show of admiration, three other first ladies attended her funeral: Nancy Reagan, Rosalynn Carter, and Betty Ford.

CHAPTER TWO

A START IN POLITICS

After Harry Truman returned home from World War I and married, his life changed. It was clear to him he did not want to be a farmer. So instead, he went into business with a friend, Eddie Jacobson. They opened a haberdashery, a men's clothing store, in Kansas City. But just three years after opening, they had to close the store. In 1922, the United States was in a **recession.** Truman's business was just one of many that failed.

It was at this point that Truman began his career in **politics,** the work of the government. In November of 1922, he easily won election as judge of the eastern **district** of Jackson County, where Kansas City is located. In his new job, he did not work in a courtroom, hearing cases. Instead, he was an administrator who helped manage the county government. He oversaw projects like the construction of buildings and roads. As a judge, Truman soon gained a **reputation** for being honest and fair.

Truman later said that he won his first election thanks to having many relatives who lived in the county. But his early political success was really

Truman (far left) opened a men's store with his friend Edward Jacobson. It was located on 12th Street in Kansas City, Missouri.

When he had to close his store, Harry Truman was $12,000 in debt. Although it took him 15 years, he eventually paid back everything he owed.

because of the support of local Democratic Party leaders. The Democratic Party is one of the two major **political parties.**

In 1924, Truman ran again for the judge position. He lost the election because he had angered the many members of Missouri's Democratic Party who belonged to the Ku Klux Klan. The Ku Klux Klan is a secret organization that believes white people are superior to people of other races. Members of the Klan had a lot of political power in Missouri during the 1920s. They sometimes tried to scare African American families by setting fire to their property. They also tried to keep African Americans from voting. While he was a judge, Truman had spoken out against them many times when they threatened African Americans.

After losing the election, Truman took different jobs. He worked for the Automobile Club of Kansas and then for a savings and loan association. He studied law as well. In 1926, he once again won election to the office of presiding judge. By this time, the Ku Klux Klan had lost some of its power. He served in this office for eight years, from 1926 through 1934.

One huge event that took place while he was in office was the Great **Depression.** The U.S. economy fell apart. Banks and businesses closed. Many people could not find work. The people of Truman's community especially appreciated his work during the Great Depression. "During that period," Truman once said, "I had to make work projects and build roads

Truman earned a reputation for fairness when he served as presiding judge of Jackson County, Missouri, in the 1920s and early 1930s.

Harry Truman was never a great public speaker. Some Americans admired him for this very reason. They said he talked like an ordinary man.

and buildings. . ." He did this "to keep enough people employed in the county so nobody would starve."

In 1934, the leading Democrats in Kansas City asked Harry Truman to run for a seat in the U.S. Senate. Kansas City was such an important place in Missouri that it often controlled what went on in the western part of the state. To many people's surprise—given the fact he had never held anything except a county office, Truman was elected—by a quarter of a million votes! The family moved to Washington, D.C., in time for Bess and Margaret to watch Truman take his oath of office in January of 1935.

In the Senate, Truman became known as a plain but honest man who spoke his mind. One important thing he did during his first term was to help draft the Civil Aeronautics Act of 1938. This act put the nation's airlines under the control of a new office. Truman also co-sponsored the Transportation Act, which put the trucking industry under federal government control, too. When he ran for reelection in 1940, it looked for a time like he might not be chosen as the Democratic **candidate.** The governor of Missouri had decided he would run for the office. But after Truman barely won the primary, he easily won the election.

During his second term, Truman became a very important senator known to people all over the country. This was because he started an investigation of how the American military was spending its money. In 1939, World War II had broken out in Europe after Germany invaded Poland. Soon Italy and Japan

entered the war on Germany's side. Americans argued about whether the United States should fight. To be ready for any decision, the country began to prepare for war. As it turned out, it was fortunate that it did so. The Japanese bombed Pearl Harbor in Hawaii on December 7, 1941. The following day, the United States declared war on Japan.

Early in his second term, people from Truman's home state had complained to him that the army was wasting money while building Fort Leonard Wood in Missouri. Truman decided to investigate army posts all over the Midwest and the South. Driving his own car, he traveled to Florida and then on to stops in Mississippi, Texas, Nebraska, and Michigan to look

Bess Truman was a very private person. She had mixed feelings when her husband won election to the Senate. She knew she would be in the public eye and was sorry to leave their home in Missouri. "Of course I'm thrilled to be going to Washington," she said, "but I have spent all my life here on Delaware Street, and it will be a change."

FIFTEEN CENTS — MARCH 8, 1943

TIME
THE WEEKLY NEWSMAGAZINE

INVESTIGATOR TRUMAN
A democracy has to keep an eye on itself.
(U. S. at War)

VOLUME XLI — NUMBER 10

Senator Truman's investigation of military wastefulness earned him an appearance on the cover of Time *magazine in 1943. He would eventually appear on 8 more covers, and was twice named* Time's Man of the Year.

When World War II broke out, Truman joined the U.S. Army Reserves.

at army projects. When he came back, he asked the Senate to vote to establish a special committee to investigate the National Defense Program, which paid for war preparations. The committee was formed and Truman was appointed chairman.

The committee discovered that some officials had been cheating both before and during the war. They had allowed certain companies to overcharge the military for weapons. Truman was credited with saving the nation millions if not billions of dollars. Because of Truman's accomplishment, *Time* magazine ran his photo on its cover in March of 1943.

By 1944, Franklin Delano Roosevelt had already served three terms as president. During his third term, he was no longer happy with his vice president, Henry A. Wallace. He needed a new vice presidential candidate and asked Truman to run. Roosevelt knew Truman was admired by most Americans, as well as by other politicians. A vice presidential candidate with enemies would have made it more difficult for Roosevelt to win. Truman was a safe choice, and with

In 1944, President Franklin D. Roosevelt (right), who was running for his fourth term in office, asked Truman to be his vice-presidential running mate. They easily won the election.

his help, Roosevelt easily won election to a fourth term. The **inauguration** took place on January 20. The event was a solemn occasion, for the United States had been at war for more than three years.

Truman soon settled into his new job as vice president. There was not a lot for him to do. He seldom saw President Roosevelt, who was busy dealing with the war. The president also was attending secret meetings with his military advisors, who were hard at work directing the creation of an **atomic bomb.** This extremely powerful weapon would be capable of terrible destruction. Roosevelt and his aides worried that Germany was hard at work on a similar weapon. They believed the United States needed to have one to ensure that it would not lose the war.

Just as Truman began to settle into his new position, everything changed. On April 12, 1945, he spent a long day doing his job as vice president, presiding over the Senate. Just a few minutes before five o'clock in the afternoon, the Senate meeting ended. Truman then visited the office of his friend, Congressman Sam Rayburn. Rayburn had received a message asking Truman to telephone the White House immediately. When Truman called, President Roosevelt's secretary asked the vice president to go to the White House at once. When he arrived, he was taken to see President Roosevelt's wife, Eleanor. She broke the news to Truman at once: Franklin Roosevelt had died that afternoon. His health had been poor for a long time. Truman had known that. He knew it was

When Truman met with Eleanor Roosevelt after her husband's death, he asked, "Is there anything I can do for you?" Mrs. Roosevelt replied, "Is there anything we can do for *you?* . . . For you are the one in trouble now."

a possibility that FDR might die during this term, but no one had expected it to happen so soon.

Two minutes after Harry Truman learned he would be president, radios broadcast the news to the American public. All the members of Roosevelt's **cabinet** gathered at the White House. So did leaders of Congress. Truman called Bess and Margaret to come at once. At 7:09 pm, on April 12, 1945, he was sworn in as the thirty-third president of the United States.

THE DEATH OF
FRANKLIN DELANO ROOSEVELT

In January of 1945, Franklin Delano Roosevelt began his fourth term as president. He was very popular with most Americans because he had helped the nation recover from the Great Depression with what he called his "New Deal." The New Deal programs helped millions of Americans by creating jobs and providing assistance to the unemployed.

When the United States entered World War II, Roosevelt became a world leader. He met with Winston Churchill of Great Britain and Joseph Stalin of the Soviet Union. The three men planned the strategy that would help the Allies win the war against Germany, Italy, and Japan. Americans gained new admiration for Roosevelt.

What they did not realize was that his health had begun to worsen. In the early 1920s, he had been struck with a disease called polio. He spent the rest of his life in a wheelchair or using braces to help him walk. For a long time, Roosevelt's health was stable. But by his fourth inauguration, he felt tired and weak. He went to Warm Springs, Georgia, where he had established a center for people with polio. There, just three months after taking the oath of office, he died. Americans had no warning that he was so ill. They were shocked and expressed great sorrow over his death, for he had skillfully led the nation during difficult times.

★★★★★★★★★★★★★★★★★★★

CHAPTER THREE

PRESIDENT TRUMAN

Harry Truman had not had very much to do after he became vice president of the United States in January 1945. When he became president, he suddenly found himself extremely busy. He held his first cabinet meeting just minutes after being sworn in as president.

After the meeting, the secretary of war asked to speak to him in private. Truman learned then that the United States was in the process of building nuclear weapons. Also known as atom or atomic bombs, these were weapons of mass destruction, the most powerful and dangerous ever developed.

Truman felt afraid and unprepared. But he knew Americans were counting on him, and he set to work. As president, he typically woke up early in the morning. He started the day with a walk, a massage, and breakfast. He was in his office by seven o'clock each morning.

Truman planned to serve only one term as vice president, but fate changed his future when President Roosevelt died.

Harry S. Truman took the oath of office on April 12, 1945. Truman was nervous about his new leadership role. He felt that he was not prepared for such a great responsibility.

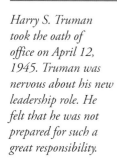

Margaret Truman was still a college student living at home when her father became president. At first she hated her new fame, but she soon learned to adjust.

U.S. relations with other countries held most of Truman's attention at the beginning of his presidency. Less than two weeks after he took the oath of office, an important meeting took place. Fifty countries gathered in San Francisco to organize the United Nations. The goals of this organization were to help maintain peace and to create better relations between countries. Truman devoted a great deal of effort to convincing voters that the United States should join. The United Nations came into being later that year, in October of 1945. The United States and most of the other 50 nations agreed to the organization's principles.

But military matters took up even more of Truman's time. When Truman became president, American involvement in World War II was already in its fourth year. Just weeks after Roosevelt died, Germany

surrendered. This meant the war was over in Europe. The Allied leaders decided to hold a meeting, called the Potsdam Conference, to discuss how to deal with defeated Germany. Truman represented the United States at Potsdam. There he met Winston Churchill, prime minister of Great Britain; and Joseph Stalin, the Soviet Union's leader. They agreed that the Allies should work together to govern Germany. They divided the country into four zones. Britain, France, the Soviet Union, and the United States would each be responsible for one zone.

President Truman met with British Prime Minister Winston Churchill (at left) and Soviet Premier Joseph Stalin (at right) at the Potsdam Conference in 1945.

Harry Truman worked very hard during his first term as president, but he never gained much popularity. Many Americans considered him dull. An expression arose to describe him that was a new twist on the popular song "I'm Just Wild about Harry." People began to say "I'm just mild about Harry," meaning they neither liked nor disliked him.

The Allied leaders at Potsdam also decided that they would demand Japan's surrender. Japan was continuing to fight in the Pacific even though it was growing weaker. Its emperor would not agree to stop fighting. Truman learned that at least 100,000 more Americans might lose their lives before Japan could be conquered. Reluctantly, he and his advisors decided that the United States should drop its atomic bombs on Japanese cities where weapons were being built. Truman hoped this would end the war and save American lives. This was a difficult decision. He knew that using the bomb would cause terrible death and destruction.

On August 6, 1945, the United States dropped an atomic bomb on the city of Hiroshima. The Japanese knew nothing of the atomic bomb. They were completely unprepared for it. The bomb destroyed more than four square miles (10 sq. km) of the city and brought death or injury to many thousands of Japanese citizens. Still, the Japanese government refused to give up. A second bomb was dropped on the city of Nagasaki three days later. After the second bomb was dropped, the emperor of Japan intervened and told his ministers that the war must be brought to an end.

By the end of World War II, new problems were developing in other parts of the world. One was the rise of **communism,** which is a system for running a government.

In communist countries, citizens do not own land and businesses. Instead, everything is owned by the government and shared by the people as a

President Truman had to make the difficult decision of whether to use the atomic bomb on Japan to help end the war. On August 6, 1945, the United States dropped an atomic bomb on the city of Hiroshima, Japan. Three days later, on August 9, another bomb was dropped on Nagasaki (left).

whole. The Soviet Union had been a communist country since 1917. Its leaders believed that all farms and factories should belong to the government. Communist leaders believed in an all-powerful state with only one political party. The Soviet people did not have elections. Also, their personal freedoms were limited. For example, they were forbidden to practice religion. After World War II, the Soviet

Much of Truman's first term was dedicated to foreign relations—the nation's dealings with other countries. Here Truman is shown talking with Madame Chiang Kai-shek, the wife of Chinese leader Chiang Kai-shek.

Union planned to spread communism to other parts of the world. It **occupied** Eastern Europe and set up communist governments in many countries there. Soon the Soviet Union became a powerful empire. This power and the communist ideals posed a threat to **democracies.**

Relations between the Soviet Union and the other Allies had begun to fall apart even before the war had ended. Afterward they became much more tense. The competitive and distrustful feelings between the Western democracies and the Soviet Union led to the Cold War.

In the Cold War, countries led by the United States and countries led by the Soviet Union never actually went to battle, but they built up supplies of nuclear weapons and were prepared to use them. Hoping to slow the spread of communism, Truman established the Truman Doctrine in 1947. This was a promise that the United States would lend support to any country threatened by communism.

President Truman was the first president to travel underwater in a modern submarine. He took a quick trip in a captured German submarine while vacationing in Key West, Florida.

President Truman kept a sign on his desk that said "The Buck Stops Here!" He once explained what it meant: "The president—whoever he is—has to decide. He can't pass the buck to anybody. No one else can do the deciding for him. That's his job."

Hiroshima, Japan,
1945

HIROSHIMA AND NAGASAKI

When Harry Truman became president, it seemed likely
that if the Allies invaded Japan, they would defeat this
powerful enemy and end World War II. But Truman knew an
invasion would cause the death of many thousands of Allied
soldiers and sailors. He decided to use the atomic bomb.

A U.S. warplane dropped the bomb on the city of
Hiroshima on August 6, 1945. The bomb exploded while
still in the air. Witnesses will remember forever the sudden
white flash. The earth shook. A cloud of dust created
darkness. In less than a minute, 70,000 buildings were
destroyed. More than 75,000 people died instantly. Another
60,000 would die before the year was over from burns,
wounds, and sickness. A few days later, a second bomb was
dropped on Nagasaki, with the same devastating effects.

At the time, many Americans expressed their belief that
Truman had done the right thing by dropping the bomb. They
praised him for having forced the Japanese to surrender.
Today, however, the bombing of Hiroshima is remembered
as one of the most horrible events in all of human history.

CHAPTER FOUR

A SECOND TERM

Harry Truman became president during a very important time in American history. Immediately, he had to become involved in foreign policy decisions that affected the entire world. But there were also problems in the United States that demanded his attention.

Toward the end of his first term, Truman was able to think more about problems at home. He knew that African American soldiers had been treated badly during and after the war. This angered him. He spoke out to encourage the government to create a new **civil rights** program. Truman wanted African Americans in the army to be treated fairly, and he wanted all African Americans to be guaranteed the right to vote. At the time, some people tried to stop black citizens from voting, especially in southern states. Truman also hoped to provide African Americans with better employment opportunities.

*Truman was able to focus more on **domestic** issues at the end of his first term.*

29

On February 1, 1865, Illinois became the first state in the nation to approve the 13th **Amendment,** *which outlawed slavery in the United States. In 1948, President Truman signed the document proclaiming February 1 as National Freedom Day.*

Throughout his life, Harry Truman loved to play the piano. When he was a teenager, he realized that he would never be good enough to earn a living as a musician. He still enjoyed playing as a hobby, however.

Truman wanted to help other Americans as well. Over time, he developed what he called his "Fair Deal" program. He wanted to help Americans by creating jobs and providing less expensive housing for people in need. He hoped to clean up the nation's slums and to provide health care to all Americans. Many members of Congress did not agree with all of President Truman's plans. They did raise the minimum wage. They also agreed that the federal government should hire people of all races rather than discriminate. But they did not go along with providing health insurance for everybody. Historians judge the Fair Deal a mixed success.

In 1948, Truman ran for election to a second term. By this time, he was not very popular with the American people. He was criticized for not getting anything done. It seemed as if the Democratic Party might not even **nominate** him as their candidate. But Truman was determined not to let that happen. He won back the support of many Democrats by taking a tough stand against their opponents, the Republicans. The president attacked the Republicans in Congress, saying they were not doing their job. He called them the "do-nothing Congress" because they had **enacted** almost no laws.

The Republicans nominated Thomas E. Dewey to run against President Truman. The race was hard-fought. Truman went all over the country to speak to Americans and ask for their votes. He delivered 275 speeches. As the election drew to a close, the polls

Before President Truman authorized other repairs to the White House, he had a balcony built on the outside of the mansion. Many Americans complained because it changed the building's appearance. But Truman really liked it, partly because it offered shade to the downstairs rooms.

President Truman had plans to help the average American. But Republicans in Congress made it difficult for him to achieve his goals. Truman (shown here addressing Congress) began to call his opponents the "do-nothing Congress."

Before all the votes were in, the early edition of the Chicago Daily Tribune *proclaimed that Thomas Dewey had won the election of 1948. But victories in California and Ohio turned the tide. Truman won the election and posed with the incorrect headline.*

The United States has governed the island of Puerto Rico since the end of the 19th century. In 1950, two Puerto Rican men attempted to **assassinate** President Truman. They wanted to advance the cause for Puerto Rican independence from the United States.

said Dewey would win. Some newspapers announced Dewey's victory before the final results were in. But Truman had actually defeated his opponent by a small number of votes. On January 20, 1949, his inauguration took place.

During Truman's second term, the world remained in turmoil. Communism continued to spread. The Soviet Union blocked all traffic in and out of the city of Berlin, hoping to place the city under communist control. Truman organized the Berlin Airlift to help the people of Berlin. Cargo planes from the United States and Great Britain brought food, coal, and other supplies to the Berliners.

In 1950, the Korean War began. Communist North Korea attacked democratic South Korea. Soon China entered the war on the side of the communists. The countries of the United Nations (UN) entered on the side of South Korea. General Douglas MacArthur commanded the UN forces. Truman and MacArthur disagreed about how to handle the war. Truman did not want the United States to become involved in a war with either the Soviet Union or China. Finally, in April of 1951, he removed MacArthur from his position. Truman believed MacArthur was making the conflict worse. The American public thought this was a terrible mistake, and Truman's popularity declined.

The fear of communism was perhaps the most talked-about issue of Truman's second term. Senator

President Truman helped establish the North Atlantic Treaty Organization (NATO), an **alliance** of North American and Western European nations.

After Soviet forces surrounded and blocked off the city of Berlin, President Truman helped organize an airlift to bring food and supplies to Berliners. This photograph shows Germans cheering a United States cargo plane as it flies over Berlin.

During the Korean War, General Douglas MacArthur (shown here with Truman in 1950) led the American and allied forces. President Truman disagreed with MacArthur's handling of the war and dismissed him in 1951. MacArthur was a beloved military hero, and Truman's popularity suffered because of the decision.

Margaret Truman had a successful career as a concert singer during her father's presidency.

Joseph McCarthy began a "witch hunt" during that time. He believed that there were many communists living in the United States and feared them. In fact, some Americans did believe that communism was a good idea. Some had joined the Communist Party. McCarthy established a Senate committee to hunt for communists. The committee accused many people, including politicians, writers, and actors, of being communists. Today historians realize that the committee made many false accusations, and that many of the people who actually did belong to the Communist Party posed no threat to American democracy. President Truman did not think well of Joseph McCarthy.

As Truman's second term approached its end, he had to decide whether to run in the next election. By this time, an amendment to the U.S. **Constitution** limited presidents to only two terms, but Truman's case was different. This new law would not take effect until the next president took office, so Truman could seek another full term. He decided against it, however. He told Americans that he would not run for a third term. "I do not think it is my duty to spend another four years in the White House," he said.

Republican Dwight D. Eisenhower, a hero from World War II, won the election of 1952. As he entered office, the Cold War with the Soviet Union continued. Both the United States and the Soviet Union built huge supplies of weapons, preparing to fight at a moment's notice. For many years, people in both countries were afraid that deadly bombs would one day cause widespread destruction and death.

This political cartoon shows the "black mark" that Joseph McCarthy was leaving on U.S. government in the early 1950s. President Truman strongly disapproved of McCarthy and his "witch-hunting."

Harry Truman enjoyed his retirement years. In 1961, he played the piano during a White House dinner given in his honor by President John F. Kennedy.

In 2004, Margaret Truman Daniel celebrated her eightieth birthday. The Trumans' only child had grown up to become a wife, mother, and writer. She wrote both history books and mystery novels.

Truman was glad to retire. He and Bess moved back to Missouri to lead a quiet life. They spent time with family and old friends. They traveled to Europe twice, where they met with such leaders as Winston Churchill and Pope Pius XII. The former president worked on writing his **memoirs,** the story of his life. He also supported Democratic candidates such as John F. Kennedy, who ran for president in 1960. On December 26, 1972, twenty years after leaving office, Harry S. Truman died at a hospital in Kansas City. He was 88 years old.

Although Truman left office as an unpopular president, his reputation has been restored in recent years. Many historians now consider him one of the greatest U.S. presidents, a man who stepped into office and worked hard to keep peace.

TRUMAN AND THE WHITE HOUSE

After World War II ended, Harry Truman had time to pay
more attention to matters at home. One thing he couldn't
help but notice was that the White House was falling apart.
Pipes leaked. Walls crumbled and even fell down. Visitors to
the second floor were lucky that the floor did not collapse
beneath them! President Truman asked Congress to set aside
an enormous amount of money to repair the president's home.

In 1948, he and his family moved to Blair House, a
mansion located nearby. Workmen removed everything
from the White House, including floors, mantels, doors, and
furniture. Only the walls were left. Inside, a new steel skeleton
was constructed. Then workers started to put the rooms
back together. The entire project took more than three years.
When the Truman family returned in March of 1952, the
White House was once more elegant, beautiful, and safe.

1880–1890	1900	1910	1920	1930

1884
Harry S. Truman is born on May 8, in Lamar, Missouri, to John and Martha Truman.

1890
The Truman family moves to Independence, Missouri.

1901
Truman graduates from high school.

1902
The Truman family moves from Independence to Kansas City. Harry goes to work for a railroad company and then for some banks.

1905
Truman joins the National Guard.

1906
Truman begins working on his family's farm.

1914
Truman's father dies. World War I begins in Europe.

1917
When the United States enters World War I, Truman joins the army and goes to fight in Europe.

1918
Truman leaves for France to fight in World War I.

1919
Truman returns from the war. After he and Bess Wallace marry, he opens a men's clothing store.

1921
Truman's business fails.

1922
Friends encourage Truman to run for county judge. He wins the election.

1924
The Trumans' only child, Margaret, is born. Harry Truman is not reelected to his post as county judge.

1926
Truman is elected county judge once again. He serves in this position through 1934.

1934
In November, Truman is elected to the U.S. Senate.

1939
World War II begins when Germany invades Poland. Great Britain, France, and the Soviet Union fight Germany and its allies.

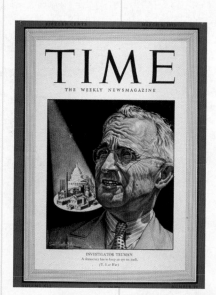

FIFTEEN CENTS   MARCH 8, 1943

TIME

THE WEEKLY NEWSMAGAZINE

INVESTIGATOR TRUMAN
A democracy has to keep an eye on itself.
(U.S. at War)

1940
Truman is reelected to the Senate.

1941
Japan bombs U.S. Navy ships at Pearl Harbor, Hawaii, on December 7. The United States enters World War II the next day, siding with Great Britain, France, and the Soviet Union. Truman heads an investigation into military spending. He learns that weapons companies have been cheating the government out of millions of dollars.

1944
Franklin Delano Roosevelt is reelected to a fourth term as president. Truman is elected vice president.

1945
On April 12, President Roosevelt dies. Truman is sworn in as the new president of the United States. In July, Truman goes to Europe to meet with other leaders at a conference at Potsdam, Germany. On August 6, he orders the atomic bomb dropped on the city of Hiroshima in Japan; a few days later, a bomb is dropped on Nagasaki. Japan surrenders on August 14.

1946
The Cold War begins after World War II as the former allies, the United States and Soviet Union, come into conflict.

1947
Truman establishes the Truman Doctrine, making a promise that the United States will help other democratic nations threatened by communism.

1948
Truman runs for reelection. Newspapers report that he has lost to Thomas E. Dewey, but Truman wins a second term. In June, the Soviet Union blocks supplies from getting to West Berlin. Truman orders the Berlin Airlift in which supplies such as food and coal are brought to the Berliners by cargo planes.

1950
The Korean War begins. American soldiers fight on the side of democratic South Korea against invaders from communist North Korea.

1951
Truman loses popularity after he removes General Douglas MacArthur from his command of troops in Korea.

1952
Truman decides not to run for reelection. Dwight D. Eisenhower wins the election in November.

1953
Harry and Bess Truman retire to Missouri, where they lead a quiet life.

1972
Harry S. Truman dies on December 26 at age 88.

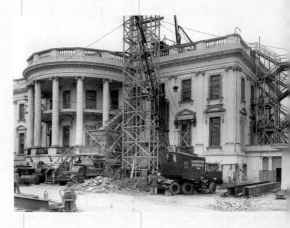

GLOSSARY

alliance (uh-LYE-uhnss) An alliance is an agreement to work together. President Truman helped establish NATO, an alliance of North American and Western European nations.

allies (AL-lize) Allies are nations that have agreed to help each other by fighting together against a common enemy. During World War II, France, Great Britain, the Soviet Union, and the U.S. were known as the Allies.

amendment (uh-MEND-ment) An amendment is a change or addition made to the U.S. Constitution or other documents. The 22nd Amendment states that no president can be elected president more than twice.

assassinate (uh-SASS-uh-nayt) To assassinate means to murder someone, especially a well-known person. Two men unsuccessfully tried to assassinate President Truman in 1950.

atomic bomb (uh-TOM-ik BAHM) An atomic bomb is a weapon that explodes with tremendous destructive power. The United States secretly developed atomic bombs during World War II.

cabinet (KAB-ih-net) A cabinet is the group of people who advise a president. Truman held his first meeting with members of his cabinet on April 12, 1945.

candidate (KAN-dih-det) A candidate is a person running in an election. In 1922, Truman was a candidate in an election for county judge.

civil rights (SIH-vel RYTZ) Civil rights are the rights guaranteed by the U.S. Constitution to all citizens of the United States. Truman encouraged the government to create a new civil rights program.

communism (KOM-yoo-niz-em) Communism is a system of government in which the central government, not the people, holds all the power. During the Cold War, a major goal of Soviet leaders was to spread communism throughout the world.

constitution (kon-stih-TOO-shun) A constitution is the set of basic principles that govern a state, country, or society. The 22nd Amendment to the U.S. Constitution was approved in 1951.

debt (DET) Debt is something that is owed. When Truman's business closed in 1921, he owed $12,000 in debt.

democracies (deh-MOK-ruh-seez) Democracies are countries in which the government is run by the people who live there. The United States is a democracy.

depression (di-PRESH-uhn) A depression is a time when businesses aren't doing well and many people become poor. When Truman was a judge, the nation was suffering through the Great Depression.

discharged (DIS-charjd) To be discharged means to be released. Truman was discharged from the army in 1919.

district (DIS-trikt) A district is a small area. Truman was a candidate in the 1922 election for judge of the eastern district of Jackson County, Missouri.

domestic (doh-MESS-tik) Domestic means having to do with the home. In politics, it refers to the affairs and issues within a country. Toward the end of Truman's first term, he was able to focus more on domestic issues.

enacted (en-AK-ted) Enacted means made from a bill into a law. Truman believed that Congress did not enact enough laws.

inauguration (ih-nawg-yuh-RAY-shun) An inauguration is the ceremony that takes place when a new president begins a term. Truman's inauguration took place on January 20, 1949.

memoirs (MEM-wahrs) Memoirs are written remembrances of one's own life. After he left the presidency, Truman wrote his memoirs.

nominate (NOM-ih-nayt) When a political party nominates someone, it chooses that person to run for a political office. Truman worried that Democrats might not nominate him for the election of 1948.

occupied (AHK-yeh-pied) An occupied area or country is one that has been taken over by another country. The Soviet Union occupied Eastern Europe after World War II.

officer (AW-fih-ser) An officer is a leader in the military who commands other soldiers. Truman was an officer in the U.S. Army.

political parties (puh-LIT-ih-kul PAR-teez) Political parties are groups of people who share similar ideas about how to run a government. Truman was a member of the Democratic political party.

politician (pawl-uh-TISH-un) A politician is a person who holds an office in government. Truman was a politician.

politics (PAWL-uh-tiks) Politics refers to the actions and practices of the government. Truman began his career in politics when he became a county judge in 1922.

preside (preh-ZYD) When people preside over something, they are in charge of it. The vice president presides over the Senate.

recession (ri-SESH-uhn) A recession is a time when business slows down and more people than usual are unemployed. The United States was in a recession in 1922, when Truman owned a store.

reputation (rep-yoo-TAY-shen) A person's reputation is what people in general think about his or her character. Truman had a reputation for being honest and fair.

Soviet Union (SOH-vee-et YOON-yen) The Soviet Union was a communist country that stretched from eastern Europe across Asia to the Pacific Ocean. It separated into several smaller countries in 1991.

surrendered (suh-REN-durd) If an enemy surrendered, it gave up to its enemy. Germany surrendered in 1945.

term (TERM) A term is the length of time a politician can keep his or her position by law. A U.S. president's term of office is four years.

THE UNITED STATES GOVERNMENT

The United States government is divided into three equal branches: the executive, the legislative, and the judicial. This division helps prevent abuses of power because each branch has to answer to the other two. No one branch can become too powerful.

EXECUTIVE BRANCH

PRESIDENT
VICE PRESIDENT
DEPARTMENTS

The job of the executive branch is to enforce the laws. It is headed by the president, who serves as the spokesperson for the United States around the world. The president signs bills into law and appoints important officials such as federal judges. He or she is also the commander in chief of the U.S. military. The president is assisted by the vice president, who takes over if the president dies or cannot carry out the duties of the office.

The executive branch also includes various departments, each focused on a specific topic. They include the Defense Department, the Justice Department, and the Agriculture Department. The department heads, along with other officials such as the vice president, serve as the president's closest advisers, called the cabinet.

LEGISLATIVE BRANCH

CONGRESS
Senate and
House of Representatives

The job of the legislative branch is to make the laws. It consists of Congress, which is divided into two parts: the Senate and the House of Representatives. The Senate has 100 members, and the House of Representatives has 435 members. Each state has two senators. The number of representatives a state has varies depending on the state's population.

Besides making laws, Congress also passes budgets and enacts taxes. In addition, it is responsible for declaring war, maintaining the military, and regulating trade with other countries.

JUDICIAL BRANCH

SUPREME COURT
COURTS OF APPEALS
DISTRICT COURTS

The job of the judicial branch is to interpret the laws. It consists of the nation's federal courts. Trials are held in district courts. During trials, judges must decide what laws mean and how they apply. Courts of appeals review the decisions made in district courts.

The nation's highest court is the Supreme Court. If someone disagrees with a court of appeals ruling, he or she can ask the Supreme Court to review it. The Supreme Court may refuse. The Supreme Court makes sure that decisions and laws do not violate the Constitution.

CHOOSING
THE PRESIDENT

It may seem odd, but American voters don't elect the president directly. Instead, the president is chosen using what is called the Electoral College.

Each state gets as many votes in the Electoral College as its combined total of senators and representatives in Congress. For example, Iowa has two senators and five representatives, so it gets seven electoral votes. Although the District of Columbia does not have any voting members in Congress, it gets three electoral votes. Usually, the candidate who wins the most votes in any given state receives all of that state's electoral votes.

To become president, a candidate must get more than half of the Electoral College votes. There are a total of 538 votes in the Electoral College, so a candidate needs 270 votes to win. If nobody receives 270 Electoral College votes, the House of Representatives chooses the president.

With the Electoral College system, the person who receives the most votes nationwide does not always receive the most electoral votes. This happened most recently in 2000, when Al Gore received half a million more national votes than George W. Bush. Bush became president because he had more Electoral College votes.

THE WHITE HOUSE

The White House is the official home of the president of the United States. It is located at 1600 Pennsylvania Avenue NW in Washington, D.C. In 1792, a contest was held to select the architect who would design the president's home. James Hoban won. Construction took eight years.

The first president, George Washington, never lived in the White House. The second president, John Adams, moved into the house in 1800, though the inside was not yet complete. During the War of 1812, British soldiers burned down much of the White House. It was rebuilt several years later.

The White House was changed through the years. Porches were added, and President Theodore Roosevelt added the West Wing. President William Taft changed the shape of the presidential office, making it into the famous Oval Office. While Harry Truman was president, the old house was discovered to be structurally weak. All the walls were reinforced with steel, and the rooms were rebuilt.

Today, the White House has 132 rooms (including 35 bathrooms), 28 fireplaces, and 3 elevators. It takes 570 gallons of paint to cover the outside of the six-story building. The White House provides the president with many ways to relax. It includes a putting green, a jogging track, a swimming pool, a tennis court, and beautifully landscaped gardens. The White House also has a movie theater, a billiard room, and a one-lane bowling alley.

PRESIDENTIAL PERKS

The job of president of the United States is challenging. It is probably one of the most stressful jobs in the world. Because of this, presidents are paid well, though not nearly as well as the leaders of large corporations. In 2007, the president earned $400,000 a year. Presidents also receive extra benefits that make the demanding job a little more appealing.

★ **Camp David:** In the 1940s, President Franklin D. Roosevelt chose this heavily wooded spot in the mountains of Maryland to be the presidential retreat, where presidents can relax. Even though it is a retreat, world business is conducted there. Most famously, President Jimmy Carter met with Middle Eastern leaders at Camp David in 1978. The result was a peace agreement between Israel and Egypt.

★ *Air Force One*: The president flies on a jet called *Air Force One*. It is a Boeing 747-200B that has been modified to meet the president's needs.

Air Force One is the size of a large home. It is equipped with a dining room, sleeping quarters, a conference room, and office space. It also has two kitchens that can provide food for up to 50 people.

★ **The Secret Service:** While not the most glamorous of the president's perks, the Secret Service is one of the most important. The Secret Service is a group of highly trained agents who protect the president and the president's family.

★ **The Presidential State Car:** The presidential limousine is a stretch Cadillac DTS.

It has been armored to protect the president in case of attack. Inside the plush car are a foldaway desk, an entertainment center, and a communications console.

★ **The Food:** The White House has five chefs who will make any food the president wants. The White House also has an extensive wine collection.

★ **Retirement:** A former president receives a pension, or retirement pay, of just under $180,000 a year. Former presidents also receive Secret Service protection for the rest of their lives.

F A C T S

QUALIFICATIONS

To run for president, a candidate must

- ★ be at least 35 years old
- ★ be a citizen who was born in the United States
- ★ have lived in the United States for 14 years

TERM OF OFFICE

A president's term of office is four years.
No president can stay in office for more than two terms.

ELECTION DATE

The presidential election takes place every four years on the first Tuesday of November.

INAUGURATION DATE

Presidents are inaugurated on January 20.

OATH OF OFFICE

I do solemnly swear I will faithfully execute the office of the President of the United States and will to the best of my ability preserve, protect, and defend the Constitution of the United States.

WRITE A LETTER TO THE PRESIDENT

One of the best things about being a U.S. citizen is that Americans get to participate in their government. They can speak out if they feel government leaders aren't doing their jobs. They can also praise leaders who are going the extra mile. Do you have something you'd like the president to do? Should the president worry more about the environment and encourage people to recycle? Should the government spend more money on our schools? You can write a letter to the president to say how you feel!

1600 Pennsylvania Avenue
Washington, D.C. 20500
You can even send an e-mail to: president@whitehouse.gov

BOOKS

Adams, Simon. *World War II*. New York: DK Publishing, 2004.

Barber, James. *Presidents and First Ladies*. New York: DK Publishing, 2002.

Feinstein, Stephen. *The 1950s: From the Korean War to Elvis*. Berkeley Heights, NJ: Enslow, 2006.

Foley, Michael. *Harry S. Truman*. Philadelphia: Chelsea House Publishers, 2004.

Lazo, Caroline Evensen. *Harry S. Truman*. Minneapolis: Lerner Publications, 2003.

Stanley, George E., and Meryl Henderson. *Harry S. Truman: Thirty-Third President of the United States*. New York: Aladdin, 2004.

VIDEOS

American Experience: Truman. DVD (Alexandria, VA: PBS Home Video, 2006).

The American President. DVD, VHS (Alexandria, VA: PBS Home Video, 2000).

Harry Truman. VHS (New York: A & E Home Video, 1994).

The History Channel Presents The Presidents. DVD (New York: A & E Home Video, 2005).

National Geographic's Inside the White House. DVD (Washington, D.C.: National Geographic Video, 2003).

INTERNET SITES

Visit our Web page for lots of links about Harry S. Truman and other U.S. presidents:

http://www.childsworld.com/links

Note to Parents, Teachers, and Librarians: We routinely verify our Web links to make sure they are safe, active sites—so encourage your readers to check them out!

INDEX